INTRODUCTION

Although fashions in toys change year by year, dolls h
never lost their appeal for children. As they become m
sophisticated, however, they become not only more expensi
but also easier to break. Here is a collection of attractive do
which can be easily made from inexpensive materials, many
which will be found around the house.

Acknowledgment:

The photograph of dolls from Greece on page 27 is reproduced b
permission of the Pitt Rivers Museum, University of Oxford.

how to make Dolls

by SYLVIA HALL

photographs by
JOHN MOYES

Ladybird Books Ltd
Loughborough 1978

4

WOOLLY PEOPLE

For each figure you will need:

8 pipe cleaners	cotton wool
5 elastic bands	old nylon tights
coloured felt pieces	coloured wool scraps
glue e.g. ('Bostik')	

Twist the pipe cleaners together in pairs. Twist two of the pairs together to make a body. Then bend another pair into a 'V' shape for the legs. Then pass the remaining twisted pair through the top of the body to make arms, leaving a short length of the body **X** above the arms **A** (see Fig 1).

Cut five pieces from the nylon tights about 2″ (5 cm) square. Take a ball of cotton wool about the size of a walnut and wrap it round **X** to make a head. Cover it with one of the squares and slip over an elastic band. Twist it – **C** – until it holds the nylon firmly. Trim off any extra nylon below the band. Take smaller balls of cotton wool and make the hands and feet.

Choose a bright wool for the jumper and tie the end on at the wrist. Wind it neatly up the arm, cross over onto the body and wind it down to the waist. Then wind back again up to the shoulders and continue down the other arm to the hand. Tie it to finish off.

For the boy, wind wool round the legs to make shorts and round the ankles for socks. For his hair tie 15 strands of wool, 2″ (5 cm) long, in a bundle and stick into place.

For the girl tie on some white wool at each ankle. Wind up the legs to the body. Tie a knot to finish.

Take a darker coloured wool for shoes and tie it on at the ankle, leaving an end $\frac{3}{4}''$ (2 cm) long. Wind down to the toe and back to the ankle, knotting with the other end to finish.

From coloured felt, cut out a half circle $5\frac{1}{4}''$ (13 cm) across – **B**. Cut out a small half circle for the waist as shown at **Y**. Glue on round the waist, and stick together the two straight edges.

Cut 30 strands of wool, 7″ (18 cm) long, for her hair and tie them in a bundle in the centre. Glue this on top of the head. Tie into bunches with small woollen bows of a different colour. Coat the sides of the head with glue and press down the hair. Draw on eyes and a mouth with coloured felt pens.

FIGURE 1

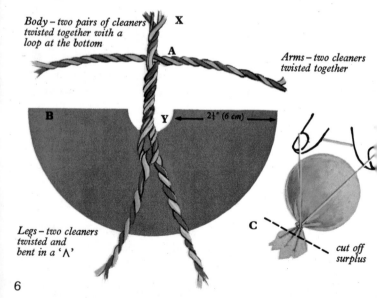

Body – two pairs of cleaners twisted together with a loop at the bottom

X

A

Arms – two cleaners twisted together

B

Y ← $2\frac{1}{4}''$ (6 cm) →

Legs – two cleaners twisted and bent in a 'Λ'

C

cut off surplus

HANKY CLOWN

You will need:

a man's handkerchief *a handful of cotton wool*
a small coloured button *some scraps of coloured*
a darning needle *wools*

Fold the handkerchief across from corner to corner as in **A** (Fig 2). Take a handful of cotton wool and make it into a ball. Push it up inside the centre of the fold and tie it round two or three times with a piece of wool – **B**. Pull up the two top corners to make arms and stitch them along the undersides with white thread – **C**. Tuck in the corners as hands and sew round them. Pull down the two legs and sew along their open edges, tucking in the corners as feet and sewing round them too.

Tie coloured wool thickly around the waist and round the wrists and ankles. Make a woollen fringe for the hair by winding wool round your fingers, tie at the centre into a bundle and cut the loops at each end – **D**.

Stitch it on top of the head. Stitch the button onto the centre of the face, and stitch two crosses for eyes and a 'V' with another colour for a mouth.

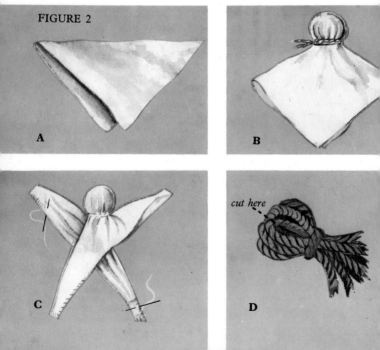

FIGURE 2

A

B

C

cut here

D

MRS MOP

You will need:

- a washing-up mop
- a man's handkerchief or square 'J' cloth
- a leg cut from old nylon tights
- a sharp craft knife
- a postcard
- a wooden spoon 12" (30 cm) long
- 3 7½" (20 cm) long pipe cleaners or wire
- blue and pink fibre-tip pens
- small yogurt carton
- 'Sellotape'

Put mop and spoon together to make a face and hair and 'Sellotape' firmly at the top and bottom of the handles. Wrap a piece of card 1¼" × 3" (3 cm × 8 cm) firmly around the top of the handles, and tape it so that it will not slip down.

Cut slits across the centre of the top of the carton as shown (Fig 3). Push the pair of handles down through the top so that the carton is above the card collar inside. This makes the body. Make a small hole on each side of the tub ½" (1 cm) from the top. Twist the three pipe cleaners together to make one and pass them through the holes for arms.

Curve them forward and cover them by binding them with strips of stocking. Start at one end and wind round until you reach the body. Stretch the stocking across the chest and then wind it down the other arm. Finish off neatly with a rubber band.

Fold the handkerchief from corner to corner. Take corner **A** and place it 4" (10 cm) above the fold **BC**. Turn the handkerchief over and wrap it around the plastic tub high under the arms. Pin it behind at **X**.

Pass corner **A** over the arm and where the stocking is stretched across the chest, tuck the handkerchief in.

Replace the pin at **X** with a few careful stitches.

Draw on eyes, nose and a mouth onto the spoon face, and trim her hair.

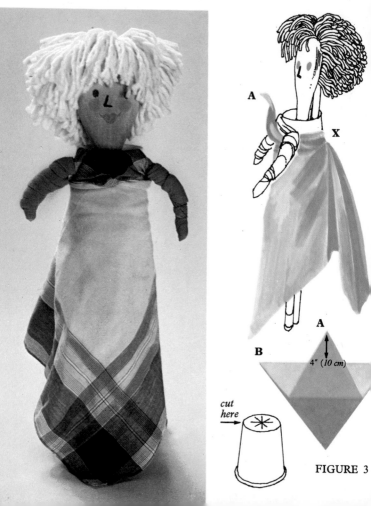

FIGURE 3

JUMP-UP JIMMY

You will need:

a stick or dowel rod 16″ (40 cm) long	old nylon tights
a piece of braid	a plastic cup or small cream tub
some buttons	some ribbon
cotton wool	glue (e.g. 'Bostik')
soap pad (e.g. 'Brillo')	16″ (40 cm) of thick yellow or red wool

Cut the foot off one leg of the tights and shorten the leg to 12″ (30 cm) (Fig 4). Tie one end of this piece with cotton, and turn it inside out. Take the cotton wool, make it into a ball and push it down into the end to make a head. Poke in the end of the stick and firmly tie round the neck with ribbon, ending with a bow.

Carefully make a round hole in the bottom of the plastic cup with the point of your scissors, and push the other end of the stick through the hole. If the plastic cup has lettering on it, scrub it clean with the soap pad. Glue the open end of the stocking round the top edge of the plastic cup, and glue braid over the join.

Choose two large buttons for eyes and a smaller one for the nose. Cut a piece of pink felt in a 'U' shape for the mouth or use a bit of thick pink wool. Glue them on.

Tie some thick red or yellow wool into loose single knots and cut them off as shown. Spread some glue on each curl and stick them to the top of the head.

Jump-up Jimmy works rather like a Jack-in-the-box.
Push the stick up and down to make Jimmy move.

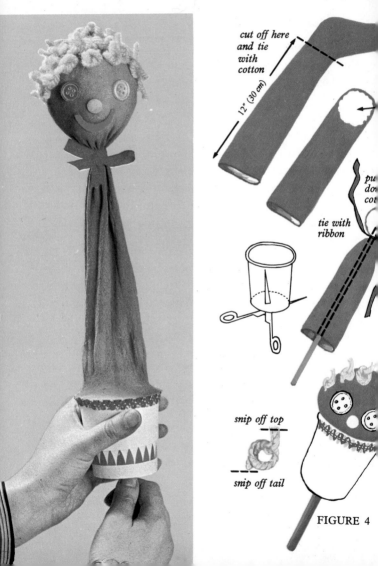

cut off here and tie with cotton

12" (30 cm)

pull down cotton

tie with ribbon

snip off top

snip off tail

FIGURE 4

GEORGE THE GUARDSMAN

You will need:

a washing-up liquid bottle 9" (23 cm) high

a toilet-roll tube

a piece of fur or fur fabric 6½" × 3" (17 cm × 8 cm)

scraps of yellow felt or thick yellow wool

black, blue and red fibre-tip pens

three pieces of red felt, one 8¼" × 7¼" (21 cm × 18 cm) for the body, a piece 4½" × 3" (11 cm × 8 cm) for the arms, and a circle 2¼" (6 cm) across for the shoulders

a postcard

glue (e.g. 'Bostik')

4" (10 cm) thick black wool

Squeeze glue around the top and bottom of the bottle. Before the glue dries, wrap the red felt around carefully so that it covers the sides completely. Then spread glue inside the long overlapping edge and stick it down.

Make a cut from the edge to the centre of the felt circle. At the centre cut a hole about ½" (1 cm) across to allow the bottle top to poke through it. Squeeze glue over the top of the bottle and stick on the felt circle.

Cut the fur to size. Spread glue around the top centimetre of the toilet-roll tube and another band of glue ¾" (2 cm) from the bottom. Before it dries, stick the fur on to make a busby. Fill in the top of the busby with a bit of fur, and stick it.

Draw eyes on with a blue pen under the edge of the fur. Cut the black wool into two 2" (5 cm) lengths for the moustache. Squeeze a thin line of glue on the face and press the moustache on. Draw on a red mouth.

Yellow wool, glued on, makes a chin-strap. Glue round the bottom edge of the roll and stick it in place on top of the body.

For the arms, cut the $4\frac{1}{2}'' \times 3''$ (11 cm × 8 cm) piece of felt from corner to corner making two triangles (Fig 5). Starting at **A** roll tightly to **B**, finally gluing it along the inside of **BC**. Snip off the pointed tops at **C**. Cut out two hands from the postcard $1'' \times 1\frac{1}{2}''$ (2·5 cm × 4 cm) as shown. Crease them along the dotted lines. Put glue on each wrist and push the hands up inside the arm rolls. Draw a rifle on a piece of $\frac{1}{2}'' \times 6''$ (1 cm × 15 cm) postcard in black.

Just above halfway up the body, glue a strip of yellow felt or wool round the waist. Spread glue on the under sides of the thinnest ends of the arms, and fix them on at shoulder level, both arms swinging forward. Bend one arm to glue the hand to the body. Glue the rifle in place.

Cut out shoulder fringes from yellow felt, and glue them on. Cut a strip from felt, and glue it across the chest. For buttons, glue on some sequins or tiny circles of card.

FIGURE 5

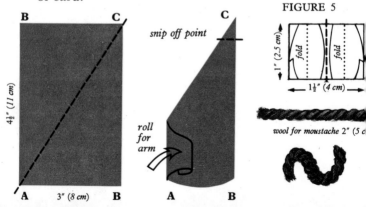

B   C

$4\frac{1}{2}''$ (11 cm)

A   3" (8 cm)   B

C

snip off point

roll for arm

A   B

1" (2.5 cm)

fold   fold

$1\frac{1}{2}''$ (4 cm)

wool for moustache 2" (5 cm)

KNITTED NANCY

You will need:

2 20g balls of pink double knitting wool	scraps of felt: pink, blue and white
5g ball of brown wool	foam chippings or kapok
no. 8 knitting needles	material 16″ × 8″
glue (e.g. 'Bostik')	(40 cm × 20 cm) for dress

For the feet, cast on 10 stitches in brown wool, and knit 6 rows in plain knitting (Fig 6). Then change to pink wool for the leg and knit 26 rows. Break off the wool and put the leg onto a spare needle. Knit other leg in the same way.

Now put the first leg onto the needles again, so there are 20 stitches altogether – **A**. Knit 12 rows right across to make the body – **B**.

FIGURE 6

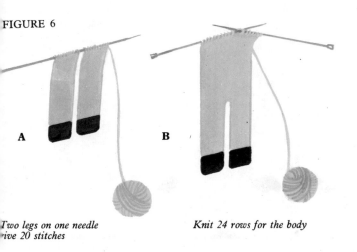

A

B

Two legs on one needle give 20 stitches

Knit 24 rows for the body

For the arms (Fig 7), cast on 25 stitches at the beginning of the next two rows – **C**. Now there are 70 stitches altogether. Knit 8 rows for the arms.

At the beginning of the next two rows cast off 2 stitches so that there are only 16 stitches left (for the neck). Knit 3 rows. Then increase 1 stitch at each end of the next two rows (there should be 20 stitches now).

Knit 12 rows for the head – **D**, then decrease 1 stitch at each end of the next 4 rows, leaving only 12 stitches. Cast these off.

Knit another shape like this in the same way. Then put the two pieces together and oversew round the edge, leaving an opening for the stuffing. Stuff the doll firmly and sew up the hole. Make running stitches all round the neck and tighten the thread slightly.

FIGURE 7

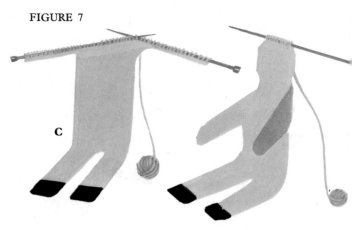

C

Cast on 25 stitches for each arm

Knit 24 rows for the head, decreasing

3" (8 cm) opening for armhole

lip shape

eye pieces

Cross over back bunch
to cover head behind

FIGURE 8

Cut the remaining brown wool into 16" (40 cm) lengths (Fig 8). Divide them into two bunches, and sew the hair along the top of the head. Cross over the back one as shown, and tie into bunches with coloured wool. Tack the bunches invisibly onto neck.

Hem round all the sides of the dress material. Fold it in half and oversew the side edges together leaving 3" (8cm) for the armholes. Make a slit 4" (10 cm) long in the centre of the folded edge. This is the head hole. Hem the edges and dress your doll. A long piece of thick wool will make a tie for the waist.

Cut out her face features from coloured felt. Glue the pink mouth onto the face. Sew a blue eye centre with a single stitch onto the eye white, then glue it onto the face.

BUZZ THE ASTRONAUT

You will need:

1 man's long, light-coloured sock

a plastic football, 5" (13 cm) across

2 pairs old nylon tights

an empty 20 cigarette packet

silver paint (poster paint or enamel)

blue and red fibre-tip pens

3 shirt buttons and a handful of cotton wool

thick, pale-coloured wool or string, 35" (90 cm) long

a craft knife

glue (e.g. 'Bostik')

2 oval stones 2¼" (6 cm) long, with flat bottoms, for feet

a white drinking straw

2 pipe cleaners

Cut the foot off the sock and cut a 4" (10 cm) slit up the ankle cuff as shown (Fig 9).

Turn it inside out, and stitch up the sides and round the top of the slit. Turn right side out again. This makes two legs.

Cut the legs and one foot off two pairs of tights. Set the foot aside, and lay the legs out flat and roll them up carefully. Push them inside the two doll's legs. Lay out flat the remainder of the two tights on top of each other and fold to make a wad of filling for the body. Push this inside and turning the raw edge over neatly, pin the top closed. Leave a gap to insert the neck later.

Take the foot of the nylon tights and pack the top firmly with the ball of cotton wool. Gather the nylon tightly to make a head and bind thread round and round the neck until it is secure. Cut off any surplus material, and attach the head to the body. Stitch firmly across the shoulders and at the neck.

FIGURE 9

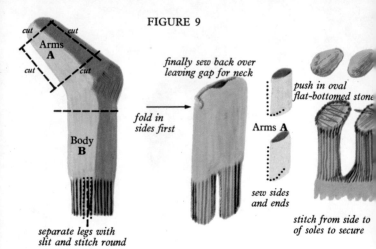

cut   cut

Arms
A

cut   cut

*fold in
sides first*

Body
B

*finally sew back over
leaving gap for neck*

*push in oval
flat-bottomed stone*

Arms **A**

*sew sides
and ends*

*separate legs with
slit and stitch round*

*stitch from side to
of soles to secure*

Glue a shirt button onto this head for a nose. Sew on the buttons for eyes and draw on a smiling mouth.

Take the foot of the man's sock – **A** – and cut along each side as shown. Use this material for the two arms. Fold the pieces in half and stitch along two edges, turn the arms inside out and stuff them with cut-up bits of the nylon tights. Finally, sew up the ends, turning in the raw edges. Sew on the arms, one straight down the side, and one out in front.

Take your two flat-bottomed stones and push them inside the bottoms of the legs. Stitch the ends to secure the stones and make the feet as shown.

For the space helmet:

If your ball is moulded with lines to show the seams in a real football, you can cut out holes for the face and neck opening on these lines as shown (Fig 10). Use a sharp knife to cut with and ask an adult to help you. Paint the ball silver.

Put in holes marked **X** with a scissor point and push in the pipe cleaners.

Knot together the ends of the piece of wool or string. Put the loop over the head and pull it down in front between the legs and up to shoulder level behind. Hook the loop into the hinge of the cigarette packet, close the lid and place it on the astronaut's back. (Any printing on the packet can be covered up with white paint or white sticky paper). Put his arms through the loops to hold the pack firm like a rucksack. Glue the straw onto the hand of the raised arm. Put on the space helmet with pipe cleaners going from the helmet, under the arms and hooked back inside the helmet to secure it to the head and shoulders.

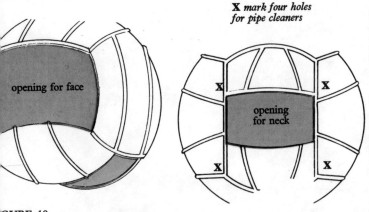

X *mark four holes for pipe cleaners*

opening for face

opening for neck

FIGURE 10

Draw a flag with blue and red pens on a small rectangle of white cotton. Stick it onto the chest.

MIRANDA THE MERMAID

You will need:

a green or blue ankle sock
scraps of blue or green felt
thick wool for hair
pink and blue fibre-tip
pens

2 10½" (27cm) squares of
white cotton material
kapok or stuffing

Draw the pattern shape (Fig 11) onto ¾" (2 cm) squared paper and cut it out. Lay the two pieces of white material one on top of the other and pin the pattern on, turning it upside down. The raised arm should be to the right. Draw a pencil line ½" (1 cm) bigger than the pattern: this is the cutting line. Cut out the material along this line.

Cut the three nicks marked under the arms and at the neck as shown. Take off the pattern, leaving the pins. Backstitch round, leaving an opening between **X** and **X**. Turn the material right side out and stuff this shape carefully, arms and head first. Pin the opening temporarily.

Draw in the features with a pencil, and then complete face with the pink pen for the mouth and nose, and blue for the eyes.

Turn the sock inside out and taper the toe by stitching 2¾" (7 cm) on each side as shown. Turn it right side out again and stuff the sock. If the sock has an elastic top, cut it off, turn in the raw edge and make a hem. Take the pins out of the body and fit it inside the sock top. Make sure Miranda is firmly stuffed.

Pin at the join of body and tail, and stitch neatly

together. A pin tuck half-way down across the back of the fish-tail will give it a curve. Cut out a fish-tail end in a different colour felt and sew it on. Cut out triangles of felt for scales and sew them on by the corners.

Tie wool into three hanks and sew them across the top of Miranda's head. Tie the hair in two bunches with coloured wool, securing them to the neck with a few stitches.

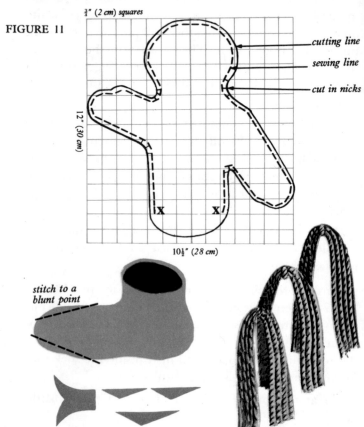

FIGURE 11

¾" (2 cm) squares

12" (30 cm)

10¼" (28 cm)

cutting line

sewing line

cut in nicks

X   X

stitch to a blunt point

DOLLS FROM GREECE

These dolls were made in Greece about 2000 years ago. They were made from clay baked in a hot oven. The arms and legs were knotted on at the shoulder and hip. For many centuries, this was the usual way to make dolls' arms and legs move. On page 37 the 'penny wood' dolls of Queen Victoria's time show a better way of making joints.

PEG DOLLS
Victorian Couple

For the man you will need:

an old-fashioned	*2 pipe cleaners*
wooden clothes peg	*black paper or black felt*
pink and black fibre-tip	*black ink and a brush*
pens	*'Plasticine'*
glue (e.g. 'Bostik')	

Paint the peg black all over except for the knob and a long 'V' in front for the shirt (Fig 12). Paint one pipe cleaner black all over except for a tip of white at each end for the hands.

Push the pipe cleaner up the centre of the peg. Bend it upwards at the back and front and bend it outward when you have reached shoulder level. Glue underneath the pipe cleaner and stick it onto the body, making sure it does not overlap the white shirt 'V'. Paint the other pipe cleaner black, cut off 2″ (5 cm), and stick this round the head as a brim for the hat.

Cut out the coat and hat patterns as shown, in black paper or felt. Glue round the inside edges **A** to **B** to make a tube. Glue inside one end of the tube and fit it on the head. Roll the coat round a pencil to curve it. Cover the inside of the top part of the coat (shaded in the diagram) with glue. Bend the arms up above the head and fix the coat in place, covering the pipe cleaner. Curl the coat tails outward by rolling them round a pencil. Bend the arms back in place again. Paint on eyes, buttons, a moustache and a coloured bow tie. Push his feet into 'Plasticine' to make him stand up.

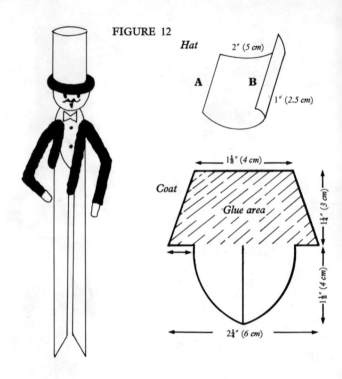

FIGURE 12

Hat

2" (5 cm)

A **B**

1" (2.5 cm)

Coat

1½" (4 cm)

Glue area

1¼" (3 cm)

1½" (4 cm)

2¼" (6 cm)

For the lady you will need:

a pipe cleaner
a piece of patterned
material 6" × 2¼"
(15 cm × 6 cm)
glue (e.g. 'Bostik')
'Plasticine'

an old-fashioned wooden
clothes peg
wool and lace edging
black and pink fibre-tip pen
'Sellotape'

Take a pipe cleaner and push it up the centre of the
peg (Fig 13). Bend the pipe cleaner half-way up toward
the head holding it firmly with your thumb and finger.
Bend it into a right angle and curve it round to the side

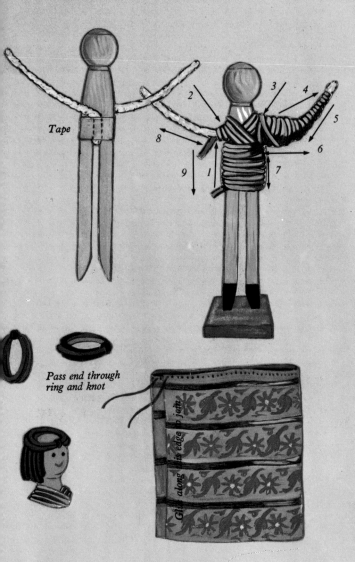

Tape

2 3 4 5
8 6
9 1 7

Pass end through ring and knot

Glue along this edge to join

FIGURE 13

of the peg as shown. Stick it onto the peg with 'Sellotape

Bind wool round the peg starting below the pip cleaner to cover it. Work up to the arms and then tak the wool over one shoulder and under the arm thre times. Repeat to cover the other shoulder. Then windin the wool tightly cover the arm to the wrist and repea winding back to the body. Winding the wool loosely, g back to half-way down the arm and return to body Move in the direction of the arrows on the diagram Take the end of the wool across the back and repeat fo the other arm, giving the effect of puffed sleeves. Win wool neatly back round the body to where you starte at the waist. Tie the wool and cut it off.

To make the skirt, join together the $2\frac{1}{4}''$ (6 cm) ends o the material by gluing. Gather round one end of the tub of material and put the peg inside it. Knot it at the wais

To make her hair, wind some wool ten times roun your finger. Remove it carefully and tie it by passing th end inside the wool ring and tying it off. Make two Glue the top of the peg and press on one of these woo bunches with the knot at the front. Put more glue on th back of the head and press on the other bunch with th knot at the top.

Take a $1\frac{1}{4}''$ (3 cm) long piece of narrow lace edgin $\frac{1}{2}''$ (1 cm) wide. Put a little glue on the hair on top of th head and at the sides. Press the lace on around the hea as a bonnet. Draw on eyes and a pink mouth an necklace. Glue on beads or sequins for buttons. Paint th tips of the peg black for feet, and push them into a thi slab of 'Plasticine'.

PEG DOLLS
Crusader and his lady

For the crusader you will need:

a clothes peg	1 pipe cleaner
silver cooking foil	gold paper from a
a postcard and paints	cigarette packet
or crayons	glue (e.g. 'Bostik')
'Plasticine'	

Make the pipe cleaner into arms in the same way as
the Victorian man (see Fig 12).

Cover each leg with a piece of silver foil 1⅓″ × 2½ (3·5 cm × 7 cm), folded in half longways and glued o Cover the body and arms by winding round long strips foil ½″ (1 cm) wide as shown (Fig 14). Start at **A** by fixin with glue and follow the arrows.

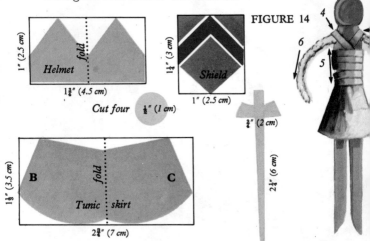

FIGURE 14

Helmet — 1″ (2.5 cm), 1¾″ (4.5 cm), fold

Cut four — ½″ (1 cm)

Shield — 1¼″ (3 cm), 1″ (2.5 cm)

¾″ (2 cm), 2¼″ (6 cm)

Tunic : skirt — 1⅓″ (3.5 cm), fold, **B**, **C**, 2¾″ (7 cm)

Glue a tunic skirt of foil round his waist and joi edges **B** and **C** with glue. Make a small pointed ball foil stuffing for the helmet. Glue it onto the head and fi a helmet-shaped piece of foil over it.

Glue together two layers of gold paper back to back to make it gold on both sides. Cut four gold circles ½ (1 cm) across from double thickness of gold paper. Stic into place on the knees and elbows of the figure. Cu out a gold sword 2¼″ (6 cm) long, and stick on a loo of wool hung round the waist as a belt. The Crusader' sword hangs from this belt.

Cut out the shield from the postcard and paint on chevron. Glue it to the arm. Draw on eyes and moustache with a pen and push the legs into a slab of 'Plasticine' to make the doll stand up.

For the lady you will need:

a clothes peg	patterned material and
2 pipe cleaners	some wool of a matching
felt 2" × 2¾"	colour
(5 cm × 7 cm)	'Plasticine'
flimsy material for veiling	

Make the arms and the body and cover them as for the Victorian lady on page 32, but without puffed sleeves. Wind the wool down to the wrists and fasten off. Make a felt hat with veiling (Fig 15). Make a fur trimming by crossing over the other pipe cleaner in front, bending it round behind the head, twisting the two ends together and tucking them away neatly below her waist.

Make running stitches round the 1¼" (3 cm) wide waist of the skirt and tie it on. Glue the long edge **A** to edge **B** of the skirt. Glue the long edges of the hat together and glue the veiling on at point **C**. Draw on her eyes, lips and hair. Glue on the hat.

FIGURE 15

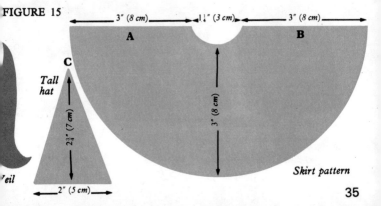

3" (8 cm) — 1¼" (3 cm) — 3" (8 cm)

A   B

C

Tall hat

2¾" (7 cm)

3" (8 cm)

2" (5 cm)

Veil

Skirt pattern

35

QUEEN VICTORIA'S PEG DOLLS

The dolls shown on these pages are peg dolls too. They were dressed by Queen Victoria when she was a young girl. She was helped by a lady and together they dressed one hundred and thirty dolls in the fashion of the day. Many of them looked like well-known people of the time and some were actors and dancers. The clothes were very neatly stitched from a great variety of different materials and many different trimmings were used.

There is, however, a difference between the Victorian peg dolls and those of today. As you can see from the

picture, the older dolls had jointed legs and arms. Our modern peg dolls have stiff legs, but their arms are made of pipe cleaners and can be moved into any position you like.

These Victorian dolls were very cheap to buy without any clothes. Just a few pence – as cheap as yours made from a clothes peg and pipe cleaner. The older ones were all hand-carved, and larger ones were made, up to 8″ (20 cm) high. Hair, mouths and eyes were all painted on. For a princess who wanted a lot of small dolls, the wooden peg doll was the best choice. By dressing them herself the young Queen Victoria created many different characters, just as you can today.

A ROMAN RAG DOLL

This rag doll was found in a Roman grave of about 300 B C. Although the cotton is rotten, and most of the sawdust and fibre stuffing has fallen out, you can see that it is just like the ones we make today.

Perhaps the face was painted on and it had some clothes on when it was new. It was probably buried with its young owner when the child died. Dolls like this have always had great appeal as they are soft and warm to cuddle (like Knitted Nancy, page 17). Naturally they become great favourites, lasting a long time, until they become too shabby even to pass on to another child.

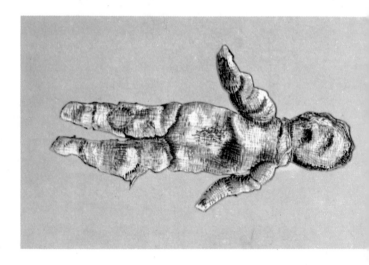

A THREE-FACED DOLL

This china doll was made in Germany about 1904.

It has one head with three faces on it, each face looking in a different direction. One is smiling, one is sleeping, and the third is crying. By turning the knob that sticks out through the top of the bonnet, the face can be changed to one with a different expression.

The bonnet fits over a cardboard hood which has on it a fringe of hair which is visible above each face. The hood conceals the other faces when they are not wanted.

This was a luxury doll for a child with very well-off parents. It could say Mama and Papa, and this was unusual in Victorian times although it is quite common day. In the pictures she is wearing a cotton petticoat but she also has a silk gown to match the bonnet.

You will need:

a white or striped pillowcase

pale coloured ribbon 1" wide × 25" long (2.5 cm × 64 cm)

yellow double knitting wool

a sheet of paper

2 pieces of pale pink material or felt, 16" × 7¾" (40 cm by 20 cm) and 7¾" × 3½" (20 cm by 9 cm)

narrow lace edging 25" (64 cm) long

kapok or stuffing

(a sewing machine would be useful)

Draw a grid of ¾" (2 cm) squares on paper and copy the patterns **A**, **B**, and **C** from Fig 16 and Fig 17. Cut round the shapes and pin down shapes **B** and **C** onto a double thickness of pink material. Cut the shapes out. Now you have two pink head pieces **C**, and two pink hand pieces **B**. Stitch the two shapes **C** round on the dotted line leaving a gap at edge **X**. Turn it right side out and stuff the head. Turn in the raw edge at **X** and stitch the neck closed.

Pin down shape **A** onto the white material. Cut it out

FIGURE 16

Squares ¾" × ¾" (2 cm × 2 cm)

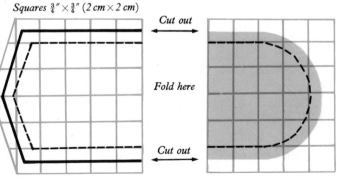

Cut out

Fold here

Cut out

A *Arms. Cut two from white material*   **B** *Hands. Cut two*

and then repeat this, making two arms. Spread out th
two arms as in diagram 1 (Fig 18), and lay the pin
hands on top. Stitch across as shown, $\frac{1}{2}"$ (1 cm) from th
edge. Then fold the arm in half longways and stitc
around the edges leaving sides **ZX** open (diagram 2)
Turn them right side out and stuff the arms, filling th
hand first, pushing the stuffing in with a long penci
Turn in the raw edges at **ZX** and stitch both arms closed

FIGURE 17

Squares $\frac{3}{4}" \times \frac{3}{4}"$ (2 cm × 2 cm)

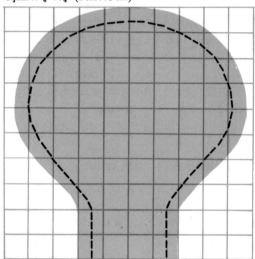

x

C *Head pattern, cut double*

Machine or handsew the lace edging onto the edg
of the ribbon. Cut off two $6\frac{1}{2}"$ (16 cm) lengths. Stitc
each one into a ring. With running stitches, gather th
ribbon and tighten each cuff round the arms. Stitch i
place.

FIGURE 18

Diagram 1

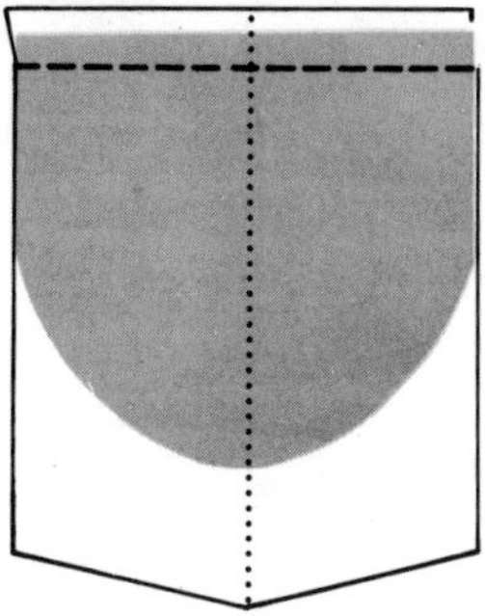

Stitch across here ½" (1 cm) from edge

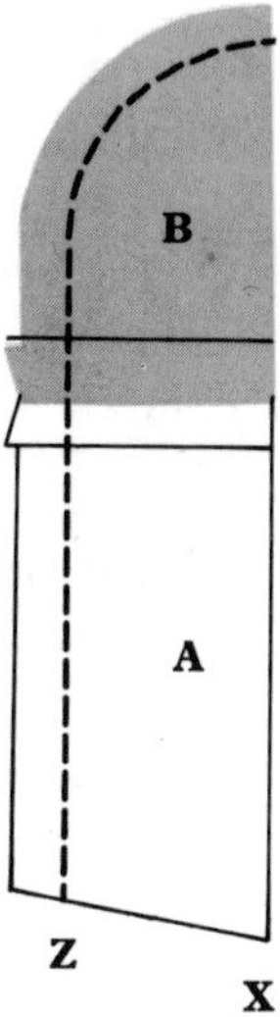

Stitch all round

B

A

Z

X

Diagram 2

Diagram 3

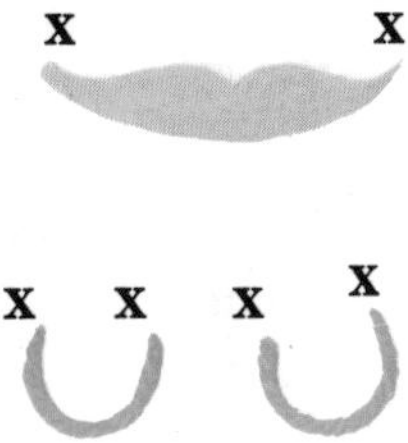

X   X

X   X   X   X

Glue on and invisibly stitch at **X**

Diagram 4

Cut 7" (18 cm) off the closed end of the pillow case. Turn it inside out and machine across this edge leaving a 3" (8 cm) gap at the centre for the neck.

Gather this edge with double thread from the right corner to the neck opening, pull it in tightly and put in a final double stitch, leaving the double thread hanging. Stitch in the same way from the left hand corner. Leave the hanging pieces of thread to gather and fit round the neck of the doll's head, one for the front and the other for the back.

Gather the 13" (32 cm) long ribbon and join it into a ring. Gather the ribbon up and sew it round the neck. Stitch the gathered neck firmly. Push the neck through the 3" (8 cm) gap and turn the pillowcase inside out. With stitches on the inside, fix the head to the bag firmly. With the pillow-case right-side out, measure 3" (8 cm) down the sides from the top of the bag and sew the arms securely onto the side seams. Cut out lips from pink felt, and two 1½" (4 cm) lengths of pale blue wool for eyelids. Glue them onto the face and secure them with invisible stitches as in diagram 3.

The curly hair is made by stitching on the yellow wool at intervals over the head, as in diagram 4. Do this with some yellow thread, making the wool loop not more than 1¼" (3 cm) long. Start by framing round the face, and then make another line of curls behind that. Continue until the head is covered down to the frill at the neck behind.

You can keep your nightdress or pyjamas inside her skirt.

CINDERELLA

CINDERELLA AND CINDERS

This is a double-ended doll. Cinders the kitchen maid can be turned over to become Cinderella all ready to go to the ball. Wide and long skirts are needed as they must cover each end of the doll in turn. A sewing machine would be useful.

You will need:

a piece of an old white sheet 16″ × 23″ (40 cm by 60 cm)

2 pieces of brightly coloured silky material 13″ × 35″ (32 cm by 90 cm) and 4¾″ × 4″ (12 cm by 10 cm)

12″ (30 cm) long bias tape to match

white material or a lace edged handkerchief for an apron

blue and pink fibre-tip pens

kapok or stuffing

10g yellow double knitting wool

yellow cotton

2 pieces of neutral coloured or checked cotton material 13″ × 35″ (32 cm × 90 cm) and 7¾″ × 6½″ (20 cm × 16 cm)

white bias tape 12″ (30 cm) long

paper for pattern

glue (e.g. Bostik)

Draw a grid of ¾″ (2 cm) squares on the paper 7″ × 12″ (18 cm × 30 cm). Copy the pattern shapes onto it from Fig 21 (on page 51), and cut them out. Double over the piece of sheet and pin the patterns on. Make sure that the fold shown in pattern **A** lies against the fold of your sheet. Cut out the pattern shapes. Then cut out another shape **A** and another shape **B**. You will now have two body shapes **A** (with a head at each end) and eight of arm shape **B**.

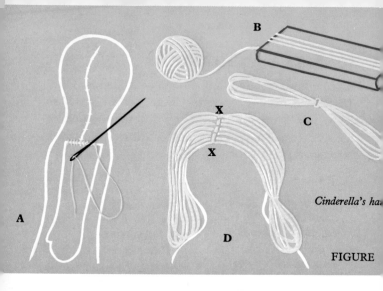

X

C

X

Cinderella's hai

A

D

FIGURE

Cut the three nicks at each side of the two necks as shown on the pattern. Pin together the two pieces of pattern **A** and sew together $\frac{1}{2}''$ (1.3 cm) from the edge. Leave a gap at **C** for the stuffing to be put in. Pin together the four pairs of pattern **B** to make four arms and sew them together. Leave a gap at **D** for the stuffing.

Turn the body and the four arms inside out and fill firmly with stuffing. Fill the heads and the hands first. Finally, sew up the stuffing holes. Sew the arms onto the sides of the shoulders as shown – **A** (Fig 19). The arms must be free to swing up and down.

Cinderella's Hair

Find a large book about 12″ (30 cm) long, and wind the yellow knitting wool round it 10 times, but not too tightly – **B**. Push it carefully off the book and tie it as shown in **C**. Make two more bunches the same way. Cut the ties and arrange the strands of wool of the three

48

bunches evenly across the top of the head, leaving loops of equal length hanging at each side – **D**.

With yellow cotton, fix the wool with a row of stitches across the top of the head – **XX**. Tie the two bunches of loops with wool and sew them to the sides of the neck invisibly. Spots of glue can be used over the head to hold the wool in position.

Use the fibre-tip pens to draw on the eyes and a happy mouth or you can make features from scraps of felt and stick them on.

Cinders' Hair

Cinders' and Cinderella's faces should be facing in opposite directions (Fig 20). Wind the yellow wool 12 times round the 12" (30 cm) long book. Push it off and tie it at the end as in **D**. Make 2 more loops like this and cut them as shown.

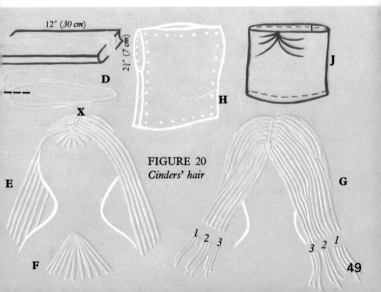

FIGURE 20
Cinders' hair

Place the three bunches on top of the head with 12″ (30 cm) lengths of wool hanging down each side – **E**.

Stitch in place invisibly at **XX**, with yellow cotton. Divide the wool at the back of the head in two equal amounts. Divide each of these into three parts. Cross over part 3 on each side as in **G**. This will help to cover the back of the head. Then start plaiting the wool on each side of the head and finish off each plait with a bow of wool.

Cut 8 pieces of wool $2\frac{1}{4}$″ (6 cm) long and tie them all together halfway along. Sew onto her forehead as a fringe – **F**.

Draw on closed eyes and a sad mouth.

Clothes

Fold the silky material in half and stitch along the 13″ (32 cm) edge. Do the same with the neutral coloured material. You will now have two tubes of material. Turn the silky material inside out so that the raw edge is on the inside. Put the silky material tube inside the other one so that the right sides of the two tubes are facing. Turn them until both seams are together. Stitch the two tubes together around one end.

Turn the neutral tube right side out so that you have one long tube with all the raw edges on the inside. Now hem both ends. Turn the silky material tube inside the neutral tube so that the right side of the silky material faces inwards. Stitch the two remaining raw edges together. This is the waist of the two skirts. Gather the waist with a running thread to fit the doll.

Cinderella's bodice is a straight piece of hemmed material gathered up at the centre front with some large stitches. Sew it into place on the body (Fig 20 – **J**).

Cinders' bodice is two pieces of material $7\frac{3}{4}'' \times 6\frac{1}{2}''$ (20 cm × 16 cm), hemmed on all sides. Place the pieces on top of each other and stitch up the sides except for the last $2\frac{3}{4}''$ (7 cm), which are left open for armholes. Seam across the shoulders except for $4''$ (10 cm) at the centre to allow for the head – **H**. Fit the bodice onto Cinders and sew it into place.

Add the double skirt now and sew the separate bias tape waistbands in place. Make a white apron for Cinders, sew on white bias tape and tie it onto the doll.

Tie tinsel and coloured wools onto Cinderella's neck and wrists.

FIGURE 21

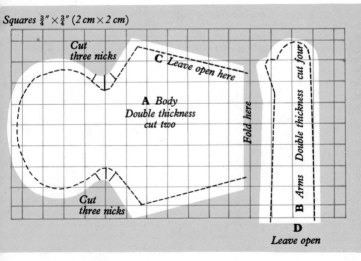

Squares $\frac{3}{4}'' \times \frac{3}{4}''$ (2 cm × 2 cm)

Cut three nicks

C Leave open here

A Body
Double thickness
cut two

Fold here

cut four

Double thickness

B Arms

Cut three nicks

D
Leave open